THE PORTAGE POETRY SERIES

Series Titles

Dear Lo
Brady Bove

Happy Everything
Caitlin Cowan

Sadness of the Apex Predator
Dion O'Reilly

The Trouble With Being a Childless Only Child
Michelle Meyer

Don't Feed the Animal
Hikari Miya

Glitter City
Bonnie Jill Emanuel

Listening to Mars
Sally Ashton

Let It Be Told in a Single Breath
Russell Thorburn

The Blue Divide
Linda Nemec Foster

Lake, River, Mountain
Mark B. Hamilton

The Watching Sky
Judy Brackett Crowe

Poetic People Power
Tara Bracco (ed.)

Talking Diamonds
Linda Nemec Foster

The Green Vault Heist
David Salner

There is a Corner of Someplace Else
Camden Michael Jones

Everything Waits
Jonathan Graham

We Are Reckless
Christy Prahl

Always a Body
Molly Fuller

Bowed As If Laden With Snow
Megan Wildhood

Silent Letter
Gail Hanlon

New Wilderness
Jenifer DeBellis

Fulgurite
Catherine Kyle

The Body Is Burden and Delight
Sharon White

Bone Country
Linda Nemec Foster

Not Just the Fire
R.B. Simon

Monarch
Heather Bourbeau

The Walk to Cefalù
Lynne Viti

Praise for

Dear Lo

"*Dear Lo* is an intimate, beautifully written poetry collection filled with vivid, dream-like imagery. It will touch the heart of anyone looking for a fresh viewpoint on our relationship to humanity."

—Tanya Taylor
author of *Why I Tell You Everything*

"I'm a voracious reader, but not of as much poetry as I'd like. I suppose it just feels too indulgent. This little luxury of *Dear Lo*, however, was a delightful reminder to allow my soul what it craves. Brady Bove dances artfully around the most relatable of feelings. Her voice is so clear and somehow familiar that you'd swear you know her."

—Alicia King
author of *Healing: The Essential Guide to Helping Others Overcome Grief & Loss*

"Brady Bove's searing, obsessive poems are deceptively simple. Beneath each poem in *Dear Lo* is a palpable urgency—the voice of a woman at a crossroads in life, desirous and searching. I was captivated from the first page and I can't wait to see what's next for this talented new poet."

—Wendy Wisner
author of *Morph and Bloom*

Dear Lo

Brady Bove

CORNERSTONE PRESS
UNIVERSITY OF WISCONSIN-STEVENS POINT

Cornerstone Press, Stevens Point, Wisconsin 54481
Copyright © 2024 Brady Bove
www.uwsp.edu/cornerstone

Printed in the United States of America by
Point Print and Design Studio, Stevens Point, Wisconsin

Library of Congress Control Number: 2023950491
ISBN: 978-1-960329-30-1

Cornerstone Press titles are produced in courses and internships offered by the
Department of English at the University of Wisconsin–Stevens Point.

DIRECTOR & PUBLISHER
Dr. Ross K. Tangedal

EXECUTIVE EDITORS
Jeff Snowbarger, Freesia McKee

EDITORIAL DIRECTOR
Ellie Atkinson

SENIOR EDITORS
Brett Hill, Grace Dahl

PRESS STAFF
Lily Alsteen, Carolyn Czerwinski, Zoie Dinehart, Sophie McPherson, Natalie Reiter

For my heart.
My own and my love.

May we all have
the calor humano
that we need.

Also by Brady Bove:

A Day of Humanity

Contents

Dear Lo

Dear Lo,

I went on a run today
around my small town—
where the snow falls,
the flowers bloom,
the sun shines,
the leaves change—
and throughout all
these seasons,
all I can think about is you.

I didn't want to run,
but the emptiness
of my house
was cooler than
the early spring
weather,
so I gave my shoes
a knowing look
and woke them from their
winter slumber.

But I don't think anyone
else was paying
you any mind.
A gaggle of women
window shopping
took one
          step
                    closer
                    to the storefront
they were eyeing
when they saw me coming.

My neon pink leggings
unsuccessful in masking

the dark, black
thoughts of you.

Those children
monkeying around
on bars a few feet
off the ground
don't even know
your name.

And the couple
in the park
with those
rows of chairs,
the flowers,
the aisle,
the pastor
waiting
can't imagine
a world
where they are
ever   apart.
You never had
a chance.

This whole town
is alive
and all I can do
is run away from
you,
and fail.
You're
my
only
companion
today.

Write What You Know

Dear Lo,

You've heard that cliché
to write what you know?
Well I guess that's
why I am here,
pen to paper,
letter by letter.
You are what I
know.

A Dandelion

Dear Lo,

Today I felt like a dandelion—
those yellow flowers
that everyone wishes
would just go away.
They do all they can
to put you down,
mow you,
cut you,
pull you out—
unwanted.

Most of the time
viewed with
disdain,
or worse,
passive
indifference
as long as you
are somewhere else.

Not in my yard,
no problem.

I blame you.

A Second Dandelion

Dear Lo,

I have more thoughts
on being a dandelion.
I used to think they
were beautiful,
bright and happy.

When I was a child,
I would pick them
and laugh
at the idea,
that even when
you put them down,
they left a mark.
Yellow pollen
on your palm,
gone but not forgotten.

But now,
everyone wants to forget
that they exist.
Their beloved homes,
their yards
reserved for only
the things they love
to grow.
Their hands
no longer yellow,
washed away
without a thought.

Pet Names

Dear Lo,

I guess I never asked…

is it okay if I call you Lo?

You can call me
whatever.

Control

Dear Lo,

I guess by now you know—
you are all I have,
and
I'm sorry
if I'm
comingoffasobsessive,
but
maybe I'm not—

not sorry
that is
becausebeingobsessedwith
you
makes me feel in

control.

And it's not like
you would ever say
no to
me.

A Reprieve

Dear Lo,

Please
I just want a reprieve.

Why do I feel
like
this black hole
I've been
sucked into
will
never end?

I keep asking
God
to show me
a—

Friend

Dear Lo,

Please.

My Garden

Dear Lo,

Did you know
I have a garden?

Crocuses,
      Irises,
            Roses—
            the loneliest
            flower.
            Every time
            I try to get
            close,
            they remind
            me of my
            mistake.
            Never
            touch a rose
            or with
            blood
            you
            will
            pay.
      Peonies,
Lilies.

Other Women

Dear Lo,

I know that I
am not the only
woman
my age
in this town.

I've even seen
a few
at work,
but even if
you wanted to
flirt
with them
you couldn't—

theysticktogether
and
don't let anyone
into their daily
lunch huddle,
not you—
not me.

I guess that means
you and I
are meant to be
forever.

Shower Thoughts

Dear Lo,

I think there is
something
in the water,
no really,
every time I shower
the water droplets
become a mirror
of you.
Like I am sitting
in a room with
300 TVs
all facing me
all showing the same exact
thing.
And even when I close
my eyes—
shampoo can be a mean
surprise—
I swear,
you're still there.

So,
I thought about you
in the shower today.

Dream Version of Me

Dear Lo,

I want to be better
than I am.
I don't want to pretend
that mediocre
is good enough.

But I also want to
practice self-love.
To be proud of where
I'm at.

To not fear the other
side of my comfort zone
or the wrong side of the bed.

I want to love life
(with good friends).

How do I be this
dream version of me
when I feel the weight
of you every time
I sleep?

My Teeth

Dear Lo,

Speaking of sleep,
did you know I grind
my teeth?

It's so frustrating,
waking up
with dawn still
resting on the dew
resting on the grass
resting on the earth,
and yet
my teeth already hurt.

I blame you
and the anxious feeling
of not knowing
when the next real
connection
will come my way,
will it be today
tomorrow
never?

For some reason
there's no in between:
it's either today
tomorrow
or
never.

My brain cannot
compute
a week
a year
a decade.

I think that's
what makes
my teeth
hurt.

My Life

Dear Lo,

I realize that I've been
a little obsessed
with telling you all
about
you.

How you are
the captain
of my mind,
how I think
about
you
all
the
time.

But yet,
I'm not sure if
I've told
you much about
my life.

About the work I
do
and how it
matters,
sometimes,
and other
times,
I'm sitting

sitting
sitting
with nothing
to do.

Praying an email
would come my way.

Trying not to think of you.

Three Letters

Dear Lo,

Your mailbox
is probably rather full
right now,
considering I've written
you
Idon'tknow
three times today
already?

And it's only 11AM.

I guess the first one
barely counts as today…
okay, 1AM is yesterday.

This is only my third letter,
we'll say.

I know what you think…

anyway,
just wanted to say,
I'm thinking about
you.
A lot.

Reflections

Dear Lo,

I don't know
whether to laugh
or cry
that in spite
of my expectations,
I met you.

One year ago,
moving here
was full of anxious
hope
of new friends
to help me cope
with being so
far from all
I've known.

Friends have
been hard to find,
but you welcomed me
that very first night.

So one year later,
as I reflect,
I don't know
whether to laugh
or cry
at the influence
you've had on
my
life.

Rainy Days

Dear Lo,

There are two types of rainy days.

The ones where everything
feels cozy, calm, cheerful.
Where you cuddle under
your sheets for an extra
five minutes
and then get up
excited
for that hot cup of tea.
Where you gather
your pillows
and blankets
and loved one(s)
and build a fort
to tell stories,
drink wine,
and have a wonderful
night.

And the ones where everything
feels damp, depressing, dour.
Where you groan and put the
pillow over your head in
frustration
because the day has started
but the last thing you want
to do is start the day.
Where you wrap yourself—
it's just you—
in a blanket with a full

bottle of wine
so you can drown your
sorrows in rain drops,
tears, and tannins.

Today is the second type of rainy day.

The Kite

Dear Lo,

I just saw someone
flying a kite,
and it looked so lonely
by itself
in the sky.

And of course,
it's a windy day
causing the whole
world to look sad
and gray.

Stupid Grass

Dear Lo,

There is no changing the
fact
that I feel like
that stupid patch of
grass
on a construction
site,
that is all alone—
just days away
from being squashed
by a new house
or shopping mall
or something
for people
with friends.

Some Time

Dear Lo,

I wish I could say
it was *good to see you*
this past weekend
when I had you all to myself.

But remember what I
said about control?

Why'd you have to
take it away
like a rug from
under
my feet?

Maybe
we should try
different things?

Like taking some time

apa   rt.

Hardly Apart

Dear Lo,

I hate to say it
but even though
we are "apart"
you still are in
my heart.

So I'll keep
writing
these stupid letters
and hide them
in a shoebox
under my
dresser.

And maybe you'll find
your way
away.

Finally Reaching Out.

Dear Lo,

I finally reached
out to those two girls
at work.

The ones
who are about
my age.

Who I've never
said more
than a curt
request
for data
or
whatever
else
you may ask
marketing.

I invited them
out for drinks,
my excuse—
to celebrate.

Because
I finally got
that certification
and I have
no one to
share the
news with,

though I didn't
tell them
that part.

I could almost
feel
you
breathing
down my neck
mocking
as I saw
the email
detailing my
success.

So.

I reached
out and now
I have to follow
through.

Here I go.

Should've Known

Dear Lo,

I should've known.
My mom told
me
4 o'clock
would be too early.

But I thought
"after work drinks"
on a Friday
would be
appropriate.

Well it's 4:45,
and
I'm alone
in this dark bar.

Time to go home.

Chuck E. Cheese

Dear Lo,

It's stupid, I know.
I felt like a
child
waiting
at
Chuck E.
Cheese
for all of her
classmates to
show.

Her mom and dad
looking concerned
in the corner,
whispering
to the manager.
Maybe we didn't
need to order all
that pizza...

is it too late to cancel?

A celebration
destined for
failure.

Curtains Drawn

Dear Lo,

On my walk home
I can't help
but think
about how that
dark
bar
reflects
the dark hole
in my heart.

The only windows
covered by curtains
of the town's favorite
football
team.

The TV
playing golf
with all those old
folks watching,
haunting.

Where are the eyes
in my heart loooking?
Captivated by mindless
scrolling
on social media—
showing those
girls I went
to high school
with, still

hanging
out in our home city,
drinks and
cheers
for their own
favorite sports teams.

And here I am,
knowing no one
outside the window
of my phone,
curtains drawn.

My Husband

Dear Lo,

Did I tell you I have
a husband?

And not one of
those men
who never understands
the importance
of what he calls
calor humano,
he's Cuban after all.

He provides the
human heat.
As we lay on the
couch,
as I cry.

I keep my tears a secret.
Because
how stupid it was
(is—I can't keep
lying to myself)
to have this
affair with
you.

When all
I have to ask
is for my husband
to hold my hand,
to go on a walk,
to be my man.

But Lo,

He's my best friend
but he cannot be
my girl
friend.

"Game Night"

Dear Lo,

I'm not sure
what I was thinking,
but I messaged
those girls
to tell
them I was
leaving the bar.

For a "low-key
game night."
They were
welcome to come.

I guess anything,
even crying,
even lying,
can be a game.

Invite

Dear Lo,

I can't believe it.
They responded.

They made it to the bar.
Just an hour
after my proposed
start.

I honestly don't know
what's worse.
Being so late
without a word
or never
showing up
at all.

They said
to come out
if I change my
mind.

So Lo,
I've got you on
speed dial
shall
we flip a coin?
Thumb wrestle?
You vs. the girls.
Who will win
this evening?

One Hour

Dear Lo,

An hour passes
slowly.

Like the end
of winter
holding on,
unready to
relinquish
to spring.

Like the last strokes
of that art
project I abandoned—
too scared
to finish
in fear it isn't
good
enough.

Like the
grandmother
driving herself
to the nursing
home,
enjoying the
freedom of the
road
one
last
time.

An hour
isn't long enough
to decide.

Go?

Dear Lo,

I'll go.

Self-Talk

Dear Lo,

What was I thinking?
Ican'tdothis.

Can I?

Putting myself out
there one more
time?

What will
they think
if I show up
unannounced?

All these
thoughts
bounce around
in my head—
anxious self-
talk—
as I walk
a few blocks
to the bar.

God bless
my legs,
they don't seem to
hear my brain.

Each thought

brings me
one
       step
             closer
                    to the bar.

Leaving

Dear Lo,

What do you think
of me once again
leaving you on
the brink
of
I'mnotsurewhat
but I
know
I'm leaving
you.

The Bar

Dear Lo,

It's the bar closest
to the river,
the river that waits only
a block away.
It's far enough
to be safe each spring
when the water
tries to avoid
you
by rising
to greet
the town,
still hibernating.
Those people, unaware that
the last of the ice melted
and maybe
they should do something
about it.

But each spring,
they feign surprise
as they stare
at telephone
lines half
submerged

and somehow
the dock
is on the other
side of the water

and everything
is wet and cold
but alive.

The bar is
far enough away
to survive
and pull
townspeople
in with a warm
place to stay—
did I mention
it's a hotel,
too?—
and a cold drink
to help
them
remember
what it means
to be alive.

The bar is partly
outdoors
so brave souls
can don
their coats
and pretend
summer is almost
here.

Live music drowns
out all thoughts of you,
for everyone but me.

Pointed

Dear Lo,

I walk up the steps slowly, heart beating.

The noise from the bar spills
over the banister and
the laughter seems
strangely
pointed
at

me.

Walking In

Dear Lo,

When I was a little girl,
I always dreamed of another world.
Full of princesses and fairy tales
where love never ever fails.

My heart would always skip a beat
when the princess's transformation was complete
when she steps into the ball at the top of the stairs
and everyone in the room turns to stare.

I feel like the princess tonight
before the godmother turned everything right,
my black jeans a dusty gown
and instead of a smile a nervous frown.

A gentleman opens the door for me...
I politely nod so he can't see
the nervousness overflowing in my eyes.
I feel sick, I would rather die.

But maybe the godmother is here after all:
I know in my heart I can no longer stall.
I lift my chin high and saunter in;
tonight will be the night I make a new friend.

There are my coworkers, but they aren't alone.
Is it really too late to go home?

Taken?

Dear Lo,

The table is
already full,
the bar
itself is about
to overflow.

panicky
panicking
panic.

But I tell myself
it's okay.
I came to be
a better me,
at least for today.

"Hey," I say,
"Is this seat taken?"

Yet

Dear Lo,

The night is wrapping up,
and I'll be honest
it was actually
kind of
fun!

There was one
who was
especially kind.
He asked me
questions
about my life.

Making me feel
welcome,
interesting,
appreciated.

I'm not sure
if you
should worry

yet.

Cheap Beer

Dear Lo,

On nights like this
it's not hard to
keep drinking
cheap beer
in the search
of free laughter
and comfort
to the point
of not
caring to
remember
the fear
of
lo-
the fear
of
you.

Lessons

Dear Lo,

I used to say that
I learn something new
every day.

I even had a log
to track the little
lessons
along the way.

Lessons from
my favorite class,
a random commercial,
some stranger that I passed.

But then, one day,
I gave you all the space
in my brain
that was once reserved
for these daily
bouts of
enlightenment.

I'm clearing
a shelf,
time to start a new log.

I'll start with this:
today I learned:
spring cleaning
does not just
have to occur
in the
spring.

Spring Cleaning

Dear Lo,

The first rule of spring cleaning:
you have to know what you have
before you can throw it away.

Just like when you have a problem,
you can't get past it
if you don't name it.

So, I guess it's time I give
my obsession a name,
time I give you
back your name.

So…

Dear Loneliness,
Welcome to spring cleaning.

Be Good

Dear Loneliness,

You know the first bloom
after a long winter?
The one you don't ever
see coming,
so stuck in the idea
of cold wind
and snow
and darkness
and when that
flower throws its petals
to the sky
proclaiming
I'm here
you realize
that there is
peace
in your
heart,
finally.

Thank you
for making me
realize
that I don't need
to be perfect
to be good.

That the flowers are
the prettiest
after the harshest

winters
and that you
have a place
in my life
so that I can
get out of my
comfort zone
and walk into
a bar.

Two Kites

Dear Loneliness,

I lied.

That day I told you
about the kite in
the sky.

Right after I noticed
the grayness
of life,
another kite
popped up
over the tree
line.

So the first one
was never
alone.

And their
flashing colors
reminded me
of the plumage
of birds
and suddenly,
though I hated
to admit it,
I guess
the world
wasn't so
gray
after
all.

Nor
so
lonely.

Alone

Dear Loneliness,

I was biking home
after an unexpected rain.

Dod   ging
        pudd   les
alo   ng
        the   way.

And I discovered my lesson
for the day:

Being alone and being lonely
are not the same things.

As I was biking,
the last few drizzles
landing on my coat,
I startled a rabbit,
two birds,
and a squirrel.

And I felt a peace
knowing that
I shared this world
with at least
one rabbit,
two birds,
and a squirrel.

And that
solo
ride filled my
soul.

26 Letters

Dear Loneliness,

Am I being
too repetitive?

I often feel as
if I have
nothing
new
to
say.

I mean 26
letters cannot
go too long
of a way.

So I stretch my
words to make them
last,
but sometimes
I feel as if soon
my thoughts will
lapse.

But even so,
I keep writing
to you.
I need to
get it all out,
to tell the truth.

I've learned, Loneliness,
how to stand
on my own two
feet.

To give you space
and to give myself peace.

My thoughts are not
quite done,
but before too long,
silence will take
anxiety's (and your)
place.

Golden Friend(s)

Dear Loneliness,

I haven't found the
golden friend(s)
of my dreams
with whom
I can chatter
and chit
and chat some more.

And often, I can hear
you knocking on
my door.

I wish this was
easier,
that I could flip
a switch
so you are
gone
and my
heart is full
with other,
real,
breathing
people.

Those girls
(from marketing)
still lunch without me,
but at least when I ask
they'll say yes
to my plans
a little more readily.

Therapy

Dear Loneliness,

Thank you.

In a way,
our relationship
has been like
therapy.

Confusing,
frustrating,
making me
cry at least
once a week,
but healing.

You taught me
I can be the princess
of my story,
or better yet,
the heroine.

I'm sorry,
but you're not my
hero.

There Goes the Fourth Wall

Dear Reader,

You should've
seen what happened
to walls one
two
three.

Or better yet,
what happened to
me.

Anyways,
I needed to say
that I could make
this a Christian book.

Spouting my story
of how God
never left me,
so what does
it even mean
to be lonely?

And it's true,
but I'm not
here to
counsel
to you.

I'm here
for Loneliness…

for me...
to bring
this affair
to its knees
(or at least
to a close).

To let her
know that
I will
never fully
let her go.

And

that's okay.

So, God
shall remain
in the foreground
but slightly
hidden
like a shadow
on a sunny
day.

A Friend

Dear Loneliness,

I told my
husband about
you
tonight.

He got quiet
like an
evening fire
dying out,
the last ember
in his eyes
snuffed
by the thought
of his wife
flirting
with
the likes of you.

I begged him
to listen as I
strived to show
how our
relationship
had
shifted.
You'renothingmorethanafriend.

I promise.

I can say
goodbye
whenever
my heart
likes.

The Bees

Dear Loneliness,

I had never
noticed
the bees.

f
l
o
a
t
i
n
g

above

and landing
on
the flowers—
even the lonely roses.

All this
time,
not actually

untouchable.

Move Out

Dear Loneliness,

Thank you for listening,
for lending your ear,
but soon
it'll be time
to pack up your things
and say
goodbye.

Your lease of my
brain
is coming to an
end.
You've got a month
to move out.
I'll be seeing you
my
friend.

That Stray Cat

Dear Loneliness,

In my garden
there is a stray cat
and a fountain.
The cat knows
that the garden
will always
have water
as long as that
tall, tiered
fountain
reminiscent
of the loveliest
wedding cake
remains.

And even on
days when it is
so cold
the water freezes,
the cat is there
licking the ice.
Content to be
challenged
by the cake
of a fountain.

So on days
when I am
in my garden,
I know I'm not alone.

Funny how comforting
a stray cat
can be.

My Final Thoughts on Dandelions

Dear Loneliness,

Once again,
I felt like a dandelion
today.

No matter how
many times I get
plucked out,
mowed down,
washed off of palms,
I can grow back.

I can reach for the sun
and match its brightness.

And one thing I never
thought about before,
is you never see
a dandelion

alone.

When there is one,
there are more,
ready to fight the
sun,
the lawn mowers,
the hands of
oblivion,
together.

The Last Letter

Dear Loneliness,

It is true what they say:
the sun will shine
even when you want
it to go away.

Sometimes it hides
its altruistic face,
but it is never
gone for long—

I guess I thought
you were the sun.

But I was wrong.

Lo,
you're the clouds
and you will
pass
with the next wind,
the next friend.

So,
until we meet again.

The End.

Acknowledgements

A book,
no matter how personal,
is not the work of one
alone.

This book,
though a key to my heart,
would not be in your hands
without the support,
hard-work, and love
of so many others.

Another reason why
loneliness no longer
prevails.

So while I no longer write
to Lo,
there are a few
to whom I must
continue letters.

Dear Alejandro Muñoz,
my incredible husband,
thank you for your
calor humano,
your unwavering
and calm presence
even when I was most
anxious.

Dear "Nilla Bean",
my sweet baby,
who is still unborn,
thank you for waiting

until edits are complete
to join us in this world.

Dear new friends
in this small town,
of whom there are too
many to name—
I hope you know
who you are—
thank you for
showing me that the
dark lens loneliness
put over my eyes
was not the truth,
and friendship can
be found
no matter where
we find ourselves.

Dear Marcya and Chris Bove,
my loving parents,
thank you for
listening to my broken
heart—
even when it didn't
want to speak—
and knowing exactly
how to respond.

Dear María and Alex Muñoz,
my amazing in-laws,
and friends,
Jesse Franklin and Kendra Rider,
thank you for your
support and care
as I placed the manuscript,
placed my heart,
in your hands.

Dear Rosi, Maggie, Teci Muñoz,
and Sofi Abou-Jaoudé,
my loyal sisters,
thank you for
never tiring of cover art
as I went back and forth
back and forth
back and forth.

Dear Dr. Ross Tangedal,
Director of Cornerstone Press,
thank you for
your patience with all
of my questions
and for moving things
                    forward
as I prepared for my
baby.

Dear Brett Hill,
my patient editor,
thank you for
~~editng~~ editing
this book with
almost as much
love
as I put into it.

Dear Carolyn Czerwinski,
my cover art magician,
thank you for making
beauty even when
I went forth and back
on cover ideas.

And finally…

Dear reader,
my new companion,
thank you for

forging

through the fears
loneliness imposed
on my heart,
and maybe
yours,
to a place where
even though
your hands
alone
hold this book,
there is nothing
to fear.

BRADY BOVE is the author *A Day of Humanity* (2020). Originally from Franklin, Tennessee, she earned a B.S. in biomedical engineering from the Georgia Institute of Technology in 2021, prior to moving to Prairie du Chien, Wisconsin. Her love of hiking and traveling, spending time with her family, and diving into her Catholic faith fuel her view of the world and deepen her connection with those in it.

Printed in the USA
CPSIA information can be obtained
at www.ICGtesting.com
LVHW040443290224
772928LV00008B/1118